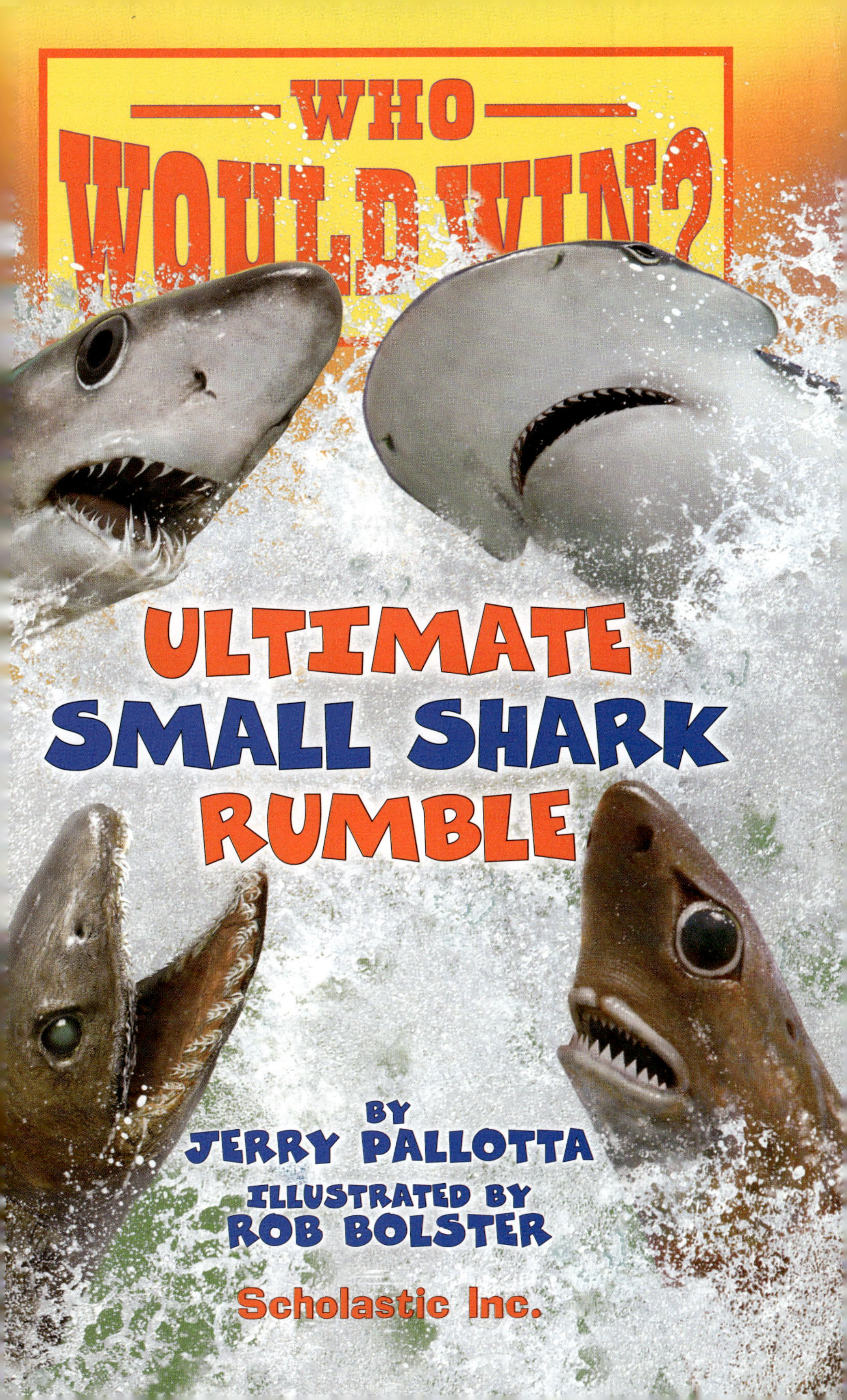
WHO
WOULD WIN?
ULTIMATE
SMALL SHARK
RUMBLE
BY
JERRY PALLOTTA
ILLUSTRATED BY
ROB BOLSTER
Scholastic Inc.

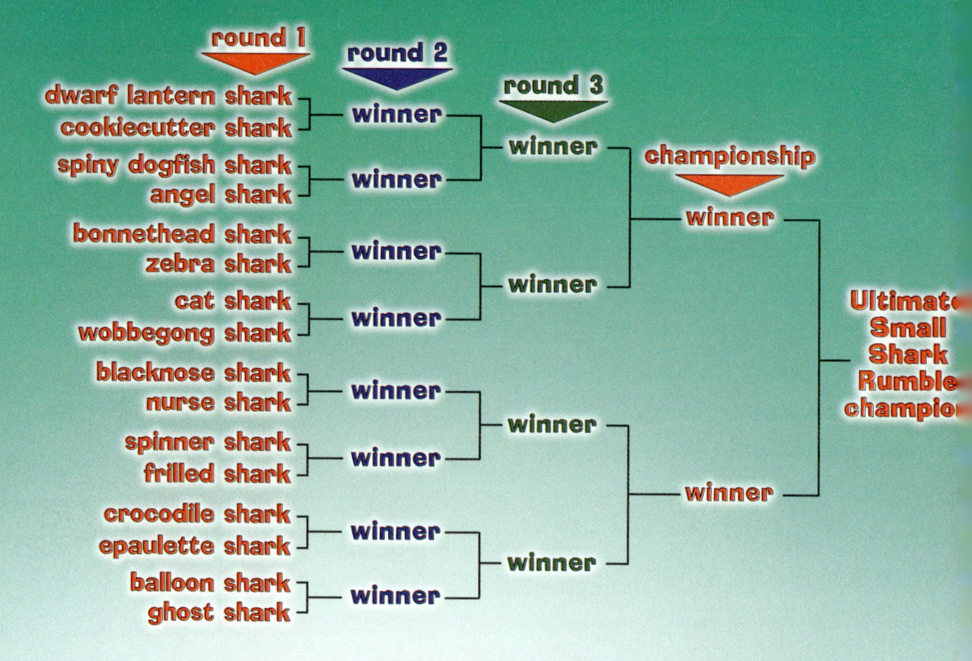

Welcome ocean cousins: Madeleine, Joey IV, Paul, Samuel, Bridgette, Judah, Evie, Iris, and, of course, Auntie Sasquatch.—J.P.

To the late "Dogfish Harry," who supplied the University of Rhode Island's Marine Biology department with dogfish specimens during the 60s and 70s.—R.B.

Library of Congress Cataloging-in-Publication Data available
ISBN 978-1-338-67220-6

10 9 8 7 6 24 25 26 27

Printed in the U.S.A. 40

First printing, 2023

We are tired of reading about big, scary sharks! What about us *small* sharks? We can be ferocious, too!

Welcome to the Ultimate Small Shark Rumble! Sixteen small sharks will meet in a bracketed battle. If a shark loses, it is out of the competition.

NAME FACT
It is called a lantern shark because it lights up.

The dwarf lantern shark, the smallest shark in the world, is only eight inches long. It lives in the deep, dark ocean and glows in the dark.

ROUND 1

DWARF LANTERN SHARK VS. COOKIECUTTER SHARK

MATCH 1

The cookiecutter shark cuts round cookie-shaped chunks out of fish and sea mammals. The cookiecutter shark is only about 18 inches long.

DID YOU KNOW?
The whale shark is the largest shark and the largest fish in the world.

SIZE FACT
This is a book about small sharks, so no more BIG facts allowed.

The cookiecutter shark swims over to the dwarf lantern shark and bites a round cookie-shaped hole. That wasn't nice, cookiecutter shark!

TOOTH FACT

When a cookiecutter shark loses a tooth, it replaces its whole row of teeth at once.

The cookiecutter shark bites the dwarf lantern shark again. The dwarf lantern shark is in trouble!

COOKIECUTTER SHARK WINS!

The spiny dogfish shark has two barbs on its back, one on each dorsal fin. These sharks travel in huge numbers. Let's just call it a dogfish.

DEFINITION
A dorsal fin is a tall triangular fin on the back of a fish or whale.

SPINY DOGFISH SHARK VS. ANGEL SHARK

The angel shark has a flat head. Its eyes are on top, and it looks like it has angel wings. This shark could be mistaken for a ray.

FACT
A tail fin is also called a caudal fin.

NO BONES
Sharks and rays are related! Neither fish has bones. Their skeletons are made of cartilage, which is the same kind of material in your nose and ears.

The angel shark hides in the sand, its favorite place. It stirs up a few clouds of sand to confuse tasty fish, crab and lobsters that may be swimming nearby.

Collective Noun
A large group of fish is called a school.

The dogfish isn't fooled by the swirling sand. It swims over and bites the angel shark. The chase is on! The larger dogfish keeps on biting the angel shark. Say your prayers, angel shark.

SPINY DOGFISH SHARK WINS!

The bonnethead shark is a small cousin to the great hammerhead shark. The bonnethead is also called a shovelhead. Would you rather be known as a hammerhead or a shovelhead?

FACT
Sharks have an up-and-down vertical tail.

TAIL TALE
Dolphins have horizontal tails.

BONNETHEAD SHARK VS. ZEBRA SHARK

An adult zebra shark has spots like a leopard but is called a zebra shark because it has stripes when it is young.

SWIMMING FACT
Most fish can swim forward or backward, or stay in one place. A shark can only swim forward.

The zebra shark is less aggressive and no match for the shifty bonnethead. The zebra shark tries to attack the bonnethead, but the bonnethead swings around and gets a good bite of the zebra shark.

SKIN FACT

Sharks have rough skin. Shark skin has "teeth" called denticles.

BONNETHEAD WINS!

The bonnethead swims on to the second round! Its great hammerhead cousins must be proud.

Cat sharks swim in shallow coastal waters as well as deep water and pose no threat to people. *Uh-oh!* Scientists say cat sharks are related to great white sharks.

LOTS OF CATS

There are more than 100 different species of cat sharks.

ROUND 1

CAT SHARK VS. WOBBEGONG SHARK

MATCH 4

This small wobbegong shark is in a group of sharks called carpet sharks. They camouflage themselves to look like the seafloor. Wobbegongs prefer to lie motionless in shallow water. They eat small fish that swim by.

ATTACK FACT

A shark that hunts by waiting for prey to swim by is called an ambush predator.

DEFINITION

An ambush is a surprise attack.

The cat shark swims over to the wobbegong. The two sharks take little bites of each other. A nip here, a nip there, then the cat shark takes a giant bite.

GOOFY FACT
Cat sharks do not meow, but they do have catlike eyes.

CAT SHARK WINS!

BOOK FACT
Should the author write a book called Cat Shark vs. Dogfish, *or is that a silly idea?*

Do not confuse a blacknose shark with a blacktip shark. The blacktip has its black mark on the top of its dorsal fin. We can only wonder why either shark has these marks.

OXYGEN FACT

Most sharks take in oxygen while swimming. Water flows through their gills.

ROUND 1

BLACKNOSE SHARK VS. NURSE SHARK

Scientists once thought that every shark had to keep swimming to survive. Then researchers discovered that nurse sharks could lie still. How do nurse sharks breathe without moving? They have spiracles, which blow seawater across their gills.

DEFINITION

Spiracles are breathing holes. Ants also have spiracles.

The quick blacknose shark swims over to the sluggish nurse shark and picks a fight. The blacknose sinks its sharp teeth into the nurse shark. *Ouch!*

COLOR FACT

Sharks blend in with the color of the ocean when you look down on them.

WHITE BELLY FACT

Most sharks have a white belly. If you scuba dive and look up, the water's surface appears to be white. Sharks are camouflaged when they swim above you.

BLACKNOSE SHARK WINS!

Today's lesson: Don't mess with a speedy shark!

'he spinner shark has a unique way of catching prey. It umps in the air, spins around, and splashes back into the cean. Jump, spin, splash! Jump, spin, splash! It is a great how. People love to watch this behavior.

JUMP FACT
When a sea creature jumps into the air, it is called breaching.

SPINNER SHARK VS. FRILLED SHARK

Meet the frilled shark. This bizarre shark is shaped like an eel, has gills on the outside of its body, and has teeth shaped ike rows of corn. Its body is not sleek and smooth like those of most sharks. Its face looks like the head of a snake!

FISH SCIENCE
Scientists who study fish are called ichthyologists.

No one wants to get bitten by a frilled shark. Its teeth are wicked scary, or should we just say frightening? The two sharks approach each other. The spinner shark breaches, spins around, and splashes down close to the frilled shark.

DENTAL FACT

When a shark loses a tooth, a new one takes its place. During its lifetime, a shark could grow thousands of new teeth!

The frilled shark is unfazed. It puts its sharp teeth into the spinner shark. The frilled shark hangs on and doesn't let go. Eventually the bleeding spinner shark gives up.

FRILLED SHARK WINS!

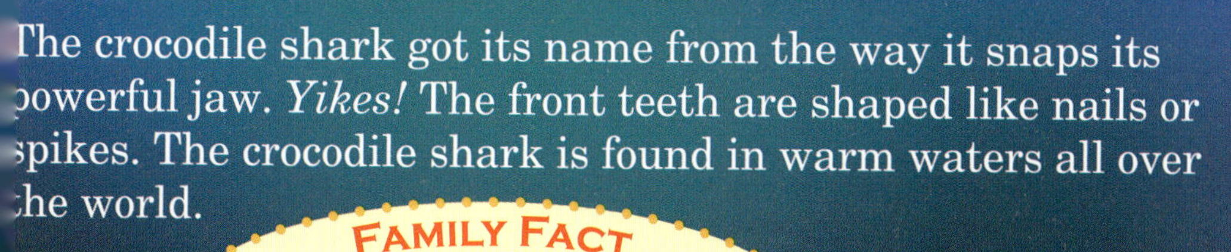
The crocodile shark got its name from the way it snaps its powerful jaw. *Yikes!* The front teeth are shaped like nails or spikes. The crocodile shark is found in warm waters all over the world.

FAMILY FACT
The crocodile shark is scientifically classified in a group called mackerel sharks.

ROUND 1

CROCODILE SHARK VS. EPAULETTE SHARK

The epaulette shark has what looks like a giant fake eyeball on each side of its body. It is another shark we don't hear much about. If you looked in its stomach, you might see it filled with crabs and sea worms.

WALKING FACT
The epaulette shark is also known as the walking shark. It uses its side fins to walk, or creep, along the ocean floor. An epaulette shark can also walk on land for a short time.

DEFINITION
An epaulette *is a shoulder ornament on a military uniform.*

The epaulette shark is no match for the crocodile shark and its long front teeth. The epaulette shark could briefly escape by walking on land. But eventually it would have to return to the ocean.

FISH FACT
Fish found in warm waters around the world are called circumtropical fish.

EYE FACT
Crocodile sharks have huge eyes.

The crocodile shark is not fooled by the fake eyes. It battles the epaulette shark. Bite, bite, *crunch, crunch*— it's all over!

CROCODILE SHARK WINS!

The balloon shark often protects itself by filling itself up with water. This makes the shark more difficult to grab. It is a clever way to fend off a predator.

BLOW FACT
Blowfish and pufferfish also blow themselves up briefly to appear larger. A bigger fish is harder to swallow.

ROUND 1

BALLOON SHARK VS. GHOST SHARK

A ghost shark is an ancient fish. It swims more with its side fins than with its tail. Modern sharks swim with their tails and steer with their side fins.

DID YOU KNOW?
A shark scientist is called a shark biologist.

GHOSTLY NAME FACT
A ghost shark is also called a ratfish and a rabbitfish.

The ghost shark swims over to the balloon shark. The ghost shark is hungry. *Oops!* What's this? All of a sudden the balloon shark is much bigger. Is this a trick?

ANOTHER NAME

A ghost shark is also called a chimaera.

The balloon shark attacks the ghost shark. The ghost shark's skinny tail isn't wide enough to help it escape in a hurry. The balloon shark gets a good chomp on the ghost shark. *Uh-oh!* The ghost shark is wounded.

BALLOON SHARK WINS!

On to the second round. There are only eight sharks left. May the best shark win!

Many readers of this book want the cookiecutter shark to win—it has such a clever name.

NON-SMOKING FACT
A cookiecutter shark is also called a cigar shark.

ROUND 2

COOKIECUTTER SHARK VS. SPINY DOGFISH SHARK

MATCH 1

The little dogfish is a tough, rugged shark. Its skin feels like sandpaper.

SPIKY FACT
Dogfish barbs look like cat claws.

FUN FACT
In the British Isles, this type of shark is called a hound.

This battle is not really a fair fight. The cookiecutter shark is smaller than the dogfish. *Wham!* The dogfish rams the cookiecutter. Then the dogfish opens its mouth and sinks its teeth into the cookiecutter!

FUN FACT
In millions of years, no shark has ever developed venomous fangs.

Cutting a little cookie out of the dogfish's side does not work this time.

SPINY DOGFISH SHARK WINS

The dogfish is on the way to the SMALL SHARK FINAL FOUR.

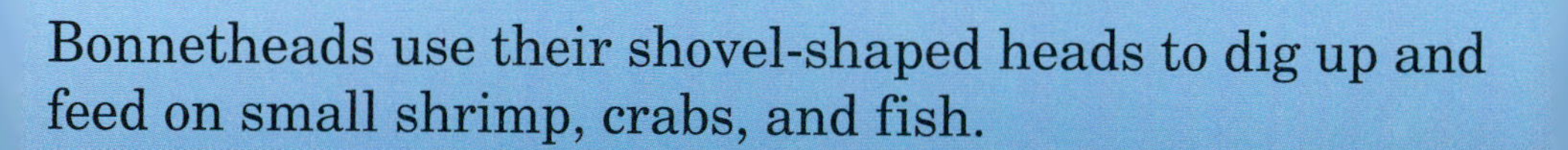

Bonnetheads use their shovel-shaped heads to dig up and feed on small shrimp, crabs, and fish.

Vegetarian Fact

A bonnethead also eats eelgrass. It is rare for any shark to eat plants. Sharks prefer meat!

BONNETHEAD SHARK VS. CAT SHARK

The cat shark is another bottom-feeder, but now it must face the bonnethead. There is no escaping!

The bonnethead forgets about eating grass and other plants. It quickly swims over to the cat shark, wanting a meaty meal. The bonnethead has better vision than the ca shark. It sees the cat shark's every move.

The cat shark shows its teeth, but the bonnethead is not impressed. The bonnethead bites the cat shark in the gills

BONNETHEAD WINS!

The blacknose shark is hoping to get itself to the next round. It has to fight the ancient frilled shark. Which shark has a more developed brain? Probably the sleek blacknose shark.

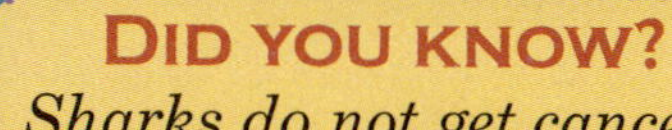

BLACKNOSE SHARK VS. FRILLED SHARK

Which shark can swim better? Probably the blacknose. Frilled sharks have lived on Earth for millions of years. It must be incredibly tough to survive that long.

DID YOU KNOW?
There are more saltwater croc attacks worldwide every year than shark attacks.

What a great matchup! Streamlined, modern-looking shark versus dinosaur-era, nasty-looking shark.

The frilled shark catches the blacknose not paying attention. The frilled shark puts a massive bite on the blacknose. Its 300 teeth really hurt.

BEACH FACT

In many beaches around the world, it is common to find shark-tooth fossils.

FRILLED SHARK WINS!

Does the crocodile shark wish it had a different name to match its long teeth? Maybe rattlesnake shark, black mamba shark, or saber-toothed-tiger shark?

ROUND 2

CROCODILE SHARK VS. BALLOON SHARK

The balloon shark wants to win the contest. Not many people have heard of a balloon shark. This is a great opportunity for fame and fortune.

THINK

What would a shark call itself if it could?

The crocodile shark shows off its teeth. They are long, pointed and impressive. *Yikes!*

The balloon shark blows itself up to appear larger. The crocodile shark slows down. Its pointed teeth are like needles. The fight is like popping a balloon.

CROCODILE SHARK WINS!

That does it! Only four sharks are left in the competition: spiny dogfish shark, bonnethead shark, frilled shark, and crocodile shark.

SMALL SHARK FINAL FOUR!

In many sports, the next round would be called the semifinals. There are only three matches left!

There is nothing flimsy about the spiny dogfish shark. It is wall-to-wall muscle. It is tough from head to tail.

OUND 3

SPINY DOGFISH SHARK VS. BONNETHEAD

The bonnethead swims with confidence. It sees the dogfish. Neither shark has ever been considered dangerous to humans.

These two sharks are about to be dangerous to each other. The dogfish swims over and bumps the bonnethead. Bump, bite! Bump, bite!

DID YOU KNOW?
Sharks often bump before they bite to see if something is worth eating.

The dogfish wears out the bonnethead.

DOGFISH SHARK WINS!

It's teeth versus teeth! Big, long, scary teeth versus hundreds of neatly arranged teeth. There is nothing pretty about these two sharks. Both sharks are scary-looking.

ROUND 3

FRILLED SHARK VS. CROCODILE SHARK

MATCH 2

If there was a crowd watching this contest, they would be chanting:
Shark! Shark! Fight! and *Fight! Fight! Shark!* Wow!

The crocodile shark swims over the frilled shark, then it swims under the frilled shark. The crocodile shark swims toward the frilled shark, then it swims away.

The crocodile shark watches how the frilled shark reacts. It sees an opening. The crocodile shark sinks its teeth into the frilled shark.

CROCODILE SHARK WINS!

The shark with the long pointed teeth wins. On to the final goes the crocodile shark!

CHAMPIONSHIP SMALL SHARK MATCH!

Uh-oh! The championship match is being played in cold water. In the ocean, there are warm water sharks and cold water sharks. The spiny dogfish shark is usually found in colder water.

SHARK TOOTH FACT

Most sharks have long pointed teeth or triangle-shaped teeth. Some triangle-shaped teeth face to the left, some face to the right.

SPINY DOGFISH SHARK VS. CROCODILE SHARK

Everyone thinks the big-toothed crocodile shark will win! Big teeth! Scary mouth! Nice jaw! The crocodile shark is used to warmer water.

The crocodile shark intends to use its long teeth to chew up the dogfish. It attacks the dogfish, but the dogfish has barbs on its dorsal fins. *Ouch!*

The cold water slows down the crocodile shark. The dogfish never slows down. It keeps on fighting, and fighting, and fighting.

This is one way the competition might have ended. Write your own ending or think of a new version of an Ultimate Rumble book.